SPRING IN THIS WORLD OF POOR MUTTS

A FRANK O'HARA AWARD BOOK

JOSEPH CERAVOLO

SPRING
IN THIS WORLD
OF POOR MUTTS

Published for the
FRANK O'HARA FOUNDATION
at Columbia University Press
New York & London 1968

To my wife & *To the tribes still singing*

THE 1968 FRANK O'HARA AWARD
FOR POETRY

The Frank O'Hara Award for Poetry, established by the Frank O'Hara Foundation, is intended to encourage the writing of experimental poetry and to aid in its publication. The annual award is named for the poet Frank O'Hara, who was killed in an automobile accident in 1966.

Few publishers are in a position to publish first volumes of poetry. A poet is often obliged to write in relative obscurity for many years without his work reaching the general public and without exercising his full influence on his time. The award is meant to carry on in some measure Frank O'Hara's interest in encouraging new poets in their work. Eligible for it are poets who have not yet had a book of poetry published or accepted for publication by a commercial or university press. Information about submitting manuscripts for the award is available from the Frank O'Hara Foundation at Columbia University Press.

The winner of the 1968 Frank O'Hara Award for Poetry is Joseph Ceravolo, who has been an important figure among young American poets since the early 1960s. Mr. Ceravolo was born on April 22, 1934, in Astoria, Queens, New York, and now lives in Bloomfield, New Jersey, with his wife Rosemary and their two children. He is a civil engineer as well as a poet. Two pamphlets of his poetry have been privately printed: *Fits of Dawn*, C Editions, 1965; and *Wild Flowers out of Gas*, Tibor de Nagy Editions, 1967.

The drawing which appears on the binding and jacket of the clothbound edition and on the cover of the paperbound edition of this book is by Donald E. Munson. The jacket and cover design is by Susan D. Tundisi.

CONTENTS

SPRING IN THIS WORLD OF POOR MUTTS

IT IS MORNING

Too late
Hard fish
Too late to be morning
Too early . . . . . early love
The tree played into
by 4 birds
The hornet . . . . . even though
the nest is shaking
Where did they go?

CAUGHT IN THE SWAMP

High is the dark clouds
and the harbor and
the egg as the antelope
frightens us through the
swampy harbor. We burn
our food, and the egg
has a seal of abandon
           in its blueness.
Which are we humming at last?
It is the running of the shiny antelope
we smell, not love.
Is it the bed?

AFTER THE RAIN

The soap is wet from the storm
and then it is lost
. . . .
I am peeking out.
I feel a chill across
the forehead
The breeze. The toy gun . . .
The quiet birds,
not as quiet as the cork

from this bottle we
drank last night

DUSK

Before the dusk grows deeper
Now comes a little moth dressed in
rose pink, wings bordered with yellow. Now
a tiger moth, now another and another   another

HEART FEELS THE WATER

The fish are staying here
and eating. The plant is
thin and has very long leaves
like insects' legs, the way
they bend down.
Through the water
the plant breaks from the water:

the line of the water and the air.
Told!

LIGHTHOUSE

All this summer fun.
The big waves, and waiting
(the moon is broken)
for the moon to come out
and revive the water. You look
and you want to watch as
men feel the beer breaking
on their lips, and women seem like
the sun on your little back.
Where are you closer to everything?
in the plants? on the photograph or
the little heart that's not
used to beating like the waves' foam?
       A wasp is
looking for a hole in the screen.
No. There's no man in the lighthouse.
There's no woman there, but there is
a light there; it is a bulb.
And I think how complete you are
in its light. Flash . . . . Flash . . . . .
. . . .
And I think of how our room
will smell; You lying on one bed
and we in the other,
facing the . . . flash . . . . .
. . . . Flash

THE WIND IS BLOWING WEST

1

I am trying to decide to go swimming,
But the sea looks so calm.
All the other boys have gone in.
I can't decide what to do.

I've been waiting in my tent
Expecting to go in.
Have you forgotten to come down?
Can I escape going in?
I was just coming

I was just going in
But lost my pail

2

A boisterous tide is coming up;
I was just looking at it.
The pail is near me
again. My shoulders have sand on them.

Round the edge of the tide
Is the shore. The shore
Is filled with waves.
They are tin waves.

Boisterous tide coming up.
The tide is getting less.

3

Daytime is not a brain,
Living is not a cricket's song.
Why does light diffuse
As earth turns away from the sun?

I want to give my food
To a stranger. I want
to be taken.
What kind of a face do

I have while leaving?
I'm thinking of my friend.

4

I am trying to go swimming
But the sea looks so calm
All boys are gone
I can't decide what to do

I've been waiting to go
Have you come down?
Can I escape

I am just coming
     Just going in

MAY

I am lost.
I had swum before.
There is no deformation fatigue
          Residual under salt water
Morning oh May flower! oh
May exist. Built.
When will water stop
cooling? Built, falling. Reeds. I am surprised.
Weakness. Torsion.
The wind, white.
Sapphire, oxidation. Million. . . . . .

WARMTH

There's nothing to love in this
rice Spring.
Collected something warm like friends.
Sail glooms are none.
Your desire
rests like sailors in
their bunks. Have beaten you, lips.
Supply me
man made keeping.
Supply it flowing out;
are brute bullets in your back
because there is
in this rice Spring

COOL BREEZE

In the night
in the day
it's possible to be defeated,
but how I love.
We walk down.
The children feel warm
but where is defeat?
I look up
The sun is
on the wet glass. The beach
where I love is now cool.
The children are still warm.

11

OCEAN

I paid you off.
    Now I want you to steal me.
My eyes are full of cement.
Wherever I am
when everything's so fated.
"I know I couldn't sleep"

Meet me wherever I am,
because I paid off,
even though I couldn't sleep.
And frighten them away.
I couldn't sleep, but a new
wave comes every few seconds.

Yes! they end on the shore.

WHITE FISH IN REEDS

Hold me
till only,   these are my
        clothes   I sit.
Give them   more songs than
the flower
These are my clothes to a
boat   Streets
have no feeling
Clouds move

Are people woman?
Who calls you
on a sun shirt sleeves down his ecstasy
The hair you are
becoming? Mmmm

That this temperate is where
I feed   The sheep sorrel flower is
And I want to
be
among all things
that bloom
Although I do not
love flowers

IN THE GRASS

Here in the grass
where the flowers
walk softer than birds
to their nest
in the clouds
Where the rain
falls toward the sky,
the small breath
of the insect
is like a breeze
before rain

HO HO HO CARIBOU

for Rosemary

I

Leaped at the caribou.
My son looked at the caribou.
The kangaroo leaped on the
fruit tree. I am a white
man and my children
are hungry
which is like paradise.
The doll is sleeping.
It lay down to creep into
the plate.
It was clean and flying.

II

Where you . . . . the axes
are. Why is this home so
hard. So much
like the sent over the
courses below the home
having a porch.

Felt it on my gate in the place
where caribous jumped
over. Where geese sons
and pouches of daughters look at
me and say "I'm hungry
daddy."   15

III

Not alone in the
gastrous   desert. We are looking
at the caribous out in the water
swimming around. We
want to go in the ocean
along the dunes.
Where do we like?
    Like little lice in the sand
we look into a fruit expanse.
Oh the sky is so cold.
We run into the water.
Lice in heaven.

IV

My heel. Ten o'clock the class.
Underwater fish
brush by us. Oh leg
not reaching!
The show is stopping
at the sky to drive in the
truck. Tell us where to
stop and eat. And
drink which comes to us out
in the sand is
                    at a star.
My pants are damp.
Is tonight treating us
but not reaching through the window.

V

Where is that bug going?
Why are your hips
rounded as the sand?
What is jewelry?

Baby sleeps. Sleeping on
the cliff is dangerous.
The television of all voice is
way far behind.
Do we flow nothing?
Where did you follow that bug
to?
    See quick . . . . . . is flying.

VI

Caribou, what have I
done? See how her
heart moves like a little
bug . . . . . . under my thumb.
Throw me deeply.
I am the floes.
Ho ho ho caribou,
light brown and wetness
caribou. I stink and
I know it.
"Screw you! . . . . you're right."

17

VII

Everyone has seen us out
with the caribou but
no one has seen us out in
the car. You passed
beyond us.
We saw your knees
but the other night we
couldn't call you.
You were more far than a
widow feeling you.
Nothing has been terrible.
We are the people who have
been running with
animals.
More than when we run?

VIII

Tell us where o eat to stop and eat.
The diner is never gonna come.
The forest things are passing.
I did drink my milk
like a mother of wolves.
Wolves on the desert
of ice cold love, of
fireproof breasts and the breast
I took like snow.
Following me
I love you
and I fall beyond
and I eat you like a
bow and arrow withering in the
        desert.

IX

No one should be mean.
Making affection and all the green
winters wide awake.
Blubber is desert. Out on
the firm lake, o firm
and aboriginal kiss.
To dance, to hunt, to sing,
no one should be mean.
Not needing these things.

X

Like a flower, little light, you open
and we make believe
we die. We die all around
you like a snake in a
well and we come up out
of the warm well and
are born again out of dry
mammas, nourishing mammas, always
holding you as I
love you and am
revived inside you, but
die in you and am
never born again in
the same place; never
stop!

RED SUN

You can't take me with a look.
These are the keys
to an orgy

after work
but they will not work
of beautiful sensuality.

Yes, work is so remote, here beneath the tides

I cannot plant the creep's
universe   As my hair stands
out   of one autumn chance
to another   O

The late red sun
farther than the equinox of a dream,
cannot make the people
more vivid than this goddess's eye.

INDIAN SUFFERING

Look, ah, dry
streets, still
not a gorged begin, he time in
you love,
cruel. What are
we doing to our faces? He waits
to grow up. Who
are you when you don't grow? Would it
mean to usually
range animal things that
satisfy? Is nature a day begun?
Bow wow wow I am
going home.
The children called
him ugly boy. I am not
afraid of
anything. Boy-not-afraid.
Ugly boy a magic.

God created his image.
I love him like the door.
Speak to me now.
Without god there is no god.
Forget everything!
Lie down and be circumscribed
            and circumcised.
Yet there is no pain.
Yet there is no joy.

NOISE OUTSIDE

I'm tired
I'm going to bed.
I'm tired. Look for me.
I will wake up
And kiss me
whether I wake up
or not.
I'm tired.
When the birds stop
I will wake up or not.
The windows are open.

WINTER SONG

I ride home.
I play.
Draw lines with me!
Draw winter with me
and the cars and the icy
arms in the drive-in.
Pull up the blanket!
Affection never rides home
with wholesale wings. They were
torrid and a baby's
voice smells like a raft.
And the river hot and blue . . . . .
is cold, evaporating
        on the screen.

WHEN THE FIRST TREE BLOSSOMS

Snow fall like April;
the icicles stick.   Like April
the birds float.
It is white foam.

Like April when the first tree blossoms
and you do not know it.

PASSIVATION

IF THE CORRODING

1

O great world that trains me! that loses my
head in the balance of coordination, even when
I'm ripe. I sting myself.

O warm world, O green ragged blood   of after dawn
as we come out singing to hear some evening birds sing.

There's no use to ask me to mind the nest,
I forget. Why do you live in the lapwing marshes?

MEDIUM REACTS WITH

2

Is there a morning moon?
A fresh wind moon?
I could hate (love)   Therefore hide me . . . . Hide . . .
going to warmness
Disease is thinking in the
sand   You were born
I am a little dirty bug
Plants!, because
I'm small   because there's no courage
in me   will you come home
with me? And
stay   With us on the bed

Like snowflakes on the ice.

26

THE METAL

3

O beautiful pale seagull who
stands near the trucks and
tractors and when they
start, looks around
surprised and turns (into whose wings open
from him) and change

Why do we invade
        as the peas are ripe as the beans
are yellow   would you forgive
            me and get up
no sooner than the lake no
sooner than

TO FORM AN ADHERENT

4

But one of you stay behind
   as a spy   because I feel more alive
      than dead   appealing as my
hide pronounces   the word
   where a bear is staying inside
and I'm beaten again
   Oh   why do I range in
      this dust spring   as you always going away
in the open
drop back while the Spring burns. . . . . . . So fresh!

PROTECTIVE COATING WHICH INHIBITS

5

Nothing has brought me back unwilling
    O   of summer
in where a pain reserves you
unripe. I choose between the excuse
   And the shocks   that pause.
When will I come here again?
When the bee makes his house larger!
When the strings let the sun alone!

Only the spring has wings. No!

FURTHER DETERIORATION OF

6

Light! light from sugar. Light
of foam accomplishing and vanish loosely
into the changed,
awake in – – – – – –
     O flower of water's vent!

Do trees repress the long birth
they lean on? Do you
bring me to my ears?
When will I
decline with the lazy starve?
into moonlight where there's no light

7

Fish, what is it like?
so let me play.
How can I
push the breeze
into the murmur of fathers?
Small and white love to flowers
not being told your
crooked bite receives me, too tame

O fish,   Am I
the bumblebee in the sun's cause?

DOUBTS

The more along you are the more

there's no ways things of passion,
the floral humaneness, can stop.

Love speeds in, struggles
in beautied temptations.

Quacks
of ducks are planed, are falling.

Are you going to hold me
or is a visionary of Spring

also coming

to take you away from me?

BEFORE IT IS DESTROYED

Before it is destroyed
all away
this love and hate
are prostrate and crippled.
I can't move its hands.
Can't move its legs.
But its lips do not
talk to Venus
about the impending end
of all lips of all kisses.
Under this bright tree
which is a symbol
of the shade and you:
I suffer as much much
as this wounded
beetle on his crazy wing
sprung together by love and a blot.

NOTHING

Nothing exists that does not empty.
Who are you feeling?
Who do you bite in the morning?
Our health
when we're sick

is the body coming.

    Our love,
a mountain fuming
    in the ocean

like a graceful race such as
black. When the shores overtake
the continent.
When the heroes are phony,
and our house less than rubble
will there be a bite, a memory still left?

FLOODS

The rain floods
the lands around.
The water bigger and bigger.
Morning warmer
and floods that my heart

O no song!
floods and floods all land.

Wet like a bird on a branch
rising in the flood

How will I wait for it
and children's bulky arms
and a woman's lips that
drip and drip.

Rain clouds bang
and water rattles.
There is no snake left.
Birds have crowned
to the tops of trees.
Buildings
to the flood splash ink.

Why is no sorrow?
When at the end of tears
and looks we're faced like
in a battleground

of a love or a dream never gotten.

I struggle to reach boat.
People around row away
from other people
thrown together like sabertooths

in a cave you have never
never been through

When someone will find you
only your tooth
sticking out of a rock

and kneels down to kiss
the only tooth he's ever found.

SCULPTURE

The dogs are barking.
I am cutting.
Am cutting like the
sounds of the sniffling
baby in the momma's
       womb. The sniffle is clean.
Now the night isn't black.
How is night not over,
cuddling us from the dark?
                (It's over)
Day has cut.
Now I have to get something.
The sun has cut
          into the dirty glass.

You are near me. The night
is rectilinear and light
in the new lipstick
on your mouth and on the colored
flowers. The irises are blue.
As far as I look we are across. A
boat crosses by. There is no monkey in me
left: sleep. There is something
sold, lemons. Corn is whizzing from the
ground. You are sleeping
and day starts its lipstick.
Where do we go from here?
Blue irises.

ROAD OF TRIALS

for Rosemary

If I went to a medicine man
I wouldn't kiss any
more, I would know my
limits. She always
erases, mentions that
just as spring is
a seal; a made
        person for any more
beatings. And I
        feel sacred in
you like the tongue.
        See, even this
animal's gamboge one.

From up north at
the long black
        trees. Over and
with all man in woods.
Yes and no, I'm
        hungry. You want
everything. Not only that
we have to
        die ferociously
in love's beary arms.
You want everything,
        everything.

But I left you and
you were prowling   around
and I thought a lot
    of things

We mustn't run away
We mustn't run away
        we have to run
    not.
        Where?
Why are all flowers
        like the snow
always in danger of food?

    When you make
            me   sad   and
            I have a smoke and
                up to my igloo lungs
    in self snotting

    I cry
    yay test hell cry of
    tubes like boiling
            meat.
    I want to touch
            you but can't

Like this horn I touch
        you   This idea
              running down my
chest, the saliva
              like this horn. This
winter light of any of
        it.   These poor women
But I'm poorer.
I'm running down and I
    find you flewing.
        Shed my skin.
I die broken loose.
In coma and I see
    you touch chest
right here right here right
        on here

        Comb and take inside me
        inside. Baby, send
        game out again. Out
        and pick up because
        not to be made
        yet as loose as it seems

Why are you the
mammal to the feeling
I have about taste?
I alias to touch
you and make ponds
breed: As mosquitoes
call you I hang on to you
and keep falling
on to your dress.

Every little thing
can't let me,
not the imported flower,
Bella cunta,   In
some quatrain of
leopard showers
I belong.   I will
look for it oh oh
from willow marks
to Ontario and
belong to your oil
or faint.

Mustn't split like
a toothpick or a
perfume in place
of tea.

In include you
like a toothpick in
a blubber heart, a seal,
see, it climbs and like
a fly it says "Hear
my skin settle!"

I love you without
knowing   love:
I'll be drawing the old man
to one side. Later saw
a bottle.

Fun Fun why are
you so near, fun
knowing love
on one side
I'll be young.

PREGNANT, I COME

I come to you
with the semen
and the babies:
ropes of the born.

I rise up as you go up
in your consciousness.
Are you unhappy
in the source?

The clouds sputter
across the ring.
Do the birds sing?

Is the baby singing in you?   yet.

BOTH CLOSE BY ME, BOTH

Come and go   see over there,
over there   wait! come!
turn out at sand,
burn with singing.
It gives away in morning;
guts
infinite pass
knives
protect from coldness,
who wants no guts now?
Should become the swim
when water
moves on the screen in
a movie   become sorry.

Summer through pleasure's floats
isn't anything.
We are going
through   This is a new city
Birds fly, wings fly;
they make bird
    fly. How can I ever get
        to this?

But we're moving out
  of the air.
    Makes better
or shark singing
So we're alone
But we're nothing out of
the air

SPRING IN THIS WORLD OF POOR MUTTS

I kiss your lips
on a grain: the forest,

the fifth, how many do
you want on here?
This is the same you
I kiss, you hear
me, you help:

I'm thirty years old.
I want to think in summer now.
Here it goes, here it's summer

(A disintegrated robot)
over us.
We are mortal. We ride
the merry-go-round. A drummer like
this is together.
Let's go feel the water.
                    Here it goes!

Again and it's morning "boom"
                    autumn
"boom" autumn
and the corn is sleeping.
It is sleeping and sweating

45

and draws the beautiful
soft green sky.

Walk home with the
animal on my shoulder
in the river, the river gets
deeper   , the Esso gets
deeper; morning,
          morning,
               cigarette,
family and animal
and parents along the river.
Oh imagination. That's how I need you.

A flying duck or an antler refrains.
The small deer at the
animal farm walks up
to us.

A waterbug comes into
the bathroom.
The north sky is all frozen over
like a river.
Like a pimple a waterbug
comes into us
and our lives are full
of rivers. Heavy waterbug!

This is the robot and he
continues across the street.

Looking at a bird
his penis is hanging down;
a wind for
its emotions.
    I don't want to sleep.
The cold around my arms.
Like an iron lung.
As sleep comes closer to the robot's
emotion. Iron.

Spring. Spring. Spring. . . . . .
        Spring!
Spring down! come down!
There it goes! there it goes!
Arm belly strike.
Press friend push.
Teeth cruel arrow. I cannot
do without,
without do I cannot, Spring.

Chrome gladly press.
Between me, my wings. Listen as
the fireflies organize.
O save me, this Spring, please!
Before I hurt her
        I hurt her only life
        too much
and it carries in this
iron bug crawling all around.
        Is this Spring?
and it carries me,
iron bug, through the Spring.   **47**

DATA

To indicate is to
turn off   in a world
away from ease.
Rotating in a mean format of oxygen.
First make and then
made all alone until
the end of a blank.
The smoke opens up and out
comes a word
in a new storage of love.
Turning off or
turning on the calcareous bases
we find our selves in
are set there by IT.
Divine and more
divine each day, no control,
but in another world.

A SONG OF AUTUMN

A dog disappears
across a small lake.
It waits for me.
It goes where I want to go.
Begins to wake up the flowers.
So leave us alone.
Because no freedom can choose
between faces and
hours as destroyed as moving,
or cold water in the
sun. I can go out
now and measure
the flies that swing around trees
like doctors around a woman
full of bars and beauties
you could never make free;
Not even if the
flowers turn to moss and
loose sensations for their stems.

AUTUMN BREAK

For who can human back?
The race, the lameness: the divine is negro,
it's white. The indian jumps from the
ridge onto the horse.
        What things are not too near us?
I see him walking away
with you, and
        the leaves keep falling
            from the trees.

LONELY IN THE PARK

A sore of love.
That I've found. Formula.
What?
From cell to cell. From play. Enzymes.

FOOTBALL

The helmets, there all alone,
the seagulls.
The one who rides.
Mother and windy, the exercise,
exercise.

TRIPOD

Since this tripod of despair is
        here alone. I am with you
    forever.
        The rag   in the tree is still there.

I LIKE TO COLLAPSE

Saturday night   I buy a soda
Someone's hand opens   I hold it
It begins to rain
Avenue A   is near the river

DOWN

The rain falls
down down and jumps
jumps in my eye
as everyone I know is sleeping

by the heaviest drops.

AUTUMN-TIME, WIND AND THE PLANET PLUTO

Like a spear afterwards
cut out,
head and eye hurts "When is he
coming to   wear me because I
am a prisoner
full of victims
and human" she said

He was the only one with
a skin disease.
Tied to, he fell "I love him"   She fell
like a stone on a rope
and instead   death instead   of arms free

Sun testicles next
of splashes

SOUL IN MIGRATION

How many sights
do I have that I'm
    against?
  A body and even the blesses are
a nuisance of man's
       glory. It is transitory;
a bird to
his mathematics and
song memory. My song's
had enough. My song is
enough plow courage;
again my soda is loud and
cares like a stable horse
out of a thunderbolt.
We're crazy men.

Out of a she
    I come to
you, shot or clubbed like
a fisherman without a fish.
Without a desperation to sing.
I want to be a servant
even though I try,
but this is backed
up for man's life, backed up.

Are these the high schools
        in our drinks?
To take us
        in a school of fish

            oh the sea, sea

            we feel

    Ah like a fish.

And we could be born
irrevocable, testament, poverty,

in the garden: Then
    only then will
I hear my son
    change toys
    at the beginning of a new day:
                a wave,
                    a splash.

DRUNKEN WINTER

> Oak oak! like like
> it then
>   cold some wild paddle
> so sky then;
> flea you say
> "geese geese" the boy
> June of winter
> of again
> Oak sky

WILD PROVOKE OF THE ENDURANCE SKY

Be uncovered!
Hoe with look life!   Sun rises.
Rice of suffering. Dawn
        in mud,
this is roof   my friend
O country   o cotton   drag
of the wild provoke,
there's a thousand years   How are
you growing?
No better to in a stranger.
Shack, village,
            brother,
wild provoke of the endurance sky!

POLAR FLOWER

Poverty needs us in
this riot
of our body,
driving the jobs of the helpless to
the grainless without weapons.
Our hopes
our bodies stay awake
in the light.
Positions, interventions, work,
riots and leaves around us.
O the hungry body
of our souls
marooned like a polar flower.

ORCHARD

Orchard sweet
sweet orchard; first
starve
    Increasing centimeter
     of air. Song
has really no meter and
  faced, remains
once. Escape into uneven   Impaired
  when it turns out.
       However possible dead
  out into wide places
my original plasma,
  oh counting birds.

       None
of unconcerns limit?
However can be made on.
Is breathing askew
but to the real sense of sign
    of describe?,
      increase "fill me"
  and disjunction.

STRUGGLING

We are going   the park.
There are swings.
There are rocks   a sand bed.
The flowers rest
the bed. The flowers
rise. We are fatigued
but invade them.
There is a smell.
It invades us.
It hides us.
Notice! there are flowers along
the bed, tiny flower clusters.
But we cannot move our legs.
We cannot move our eyes.

GROW

I fight and fight.
I wake up.
The oasis is now dark.
I cannot hear anything.

The wind is felt
and the stars and the sand
so that no one
will be taken by pain.

I sit next to the bushes,
Hercules couldn't move me,
and sleep and dream.

The sand, the stars are solid
in this sleeping oasis,
alone with the desert and
the metaphysical cigarette.

DANGERS OF THE JOURNEY TO THE HAPPY LAND

Talk of energy.   Mayan sub-flower
Come to light and feel physically intent to
plasm
     Even if I don't share
     Instance the mother
Talk of energy or stolen from her
mother
     I didn't do that for
nothing   I speak as a wife to the
capsizing   Both are once
Perspire like an autumn wind bakes. Mayan
sub-flowers.
     Am I allowed to go to
the tough section?   That's tough.
     Mayan sub-flowers in
          the shade.

RISK

It is made up of (in our latitude)
wind through an inflamed solar plexis.
The lobelias are so close to
the offbeat.
O candy for our sore,
       Lend to beggars   the
hound, the flowers in season,
the Rough Sun
       sun of the ripened
nearly concocted colder than night
        O summer

HAPPINESS IN THE TREES

O height dispersed and head
in sometimes joining
these sleeps. O primitive touch
between fingers and dawn
on the back

You are no more
simple than a cedar tree
whose children change
the interesting earth
and promise to shake her
before the wind blows
      away from you
in the velocity of rest

FLY

The lights are on;
flesh is next to the body.
Drinking out of the glass
and the tide sways
you in my arms.
A membrane of wisdom
or the lips. I spit.
Nothing is changed.
The lights are on.
The sound of the waves
        through the traffic. I rub your body.
Hold me: the waves.
A fly alights
        on the glass.
It sings a song
with a nerve impulse.
And the tide
            noticed by
the birds———— fit to eat
comes back in
the dream of a metropolis.
The flies full of
energy, full of light   alight.

THE BOOK OF WILD FLOWERS

I can't live blossoming drunk
this story of climbed up
Be world to   any apples!
be anxiously! Hurrah
the desert   Ream them! Feed them!
I can't live blossoming drunk
                    oh
chicory sun (to daughters)   dawn
to the yellow stings
to lean   frim fram   up
on   so I knoll   rushing rushing   against . . . . oh hum of dawn
against the knoll

MOUNTAINS

The surface of the mountain flows.
Here on these vibrating peaks.
I am hungry,
and the mountain continues to flow.
The light, the cylinder,
The river and the river
between the lightning and the love
and the nude river.
Next to the body, continues,
continues to drive my penis
into the seaweed forever,
today.

THE GREEN LAKE IS AWAKE

PART 1

The womb can
remind you of mosquitoes
if you imagine you are
in a carriage with a net
over it

A negro is shining the
top of a used car. The pennant
is above him.

Where are you? Here I am
crossing the street. This is
my mommy. O sun!

A dog walks over to the
little boy. He walks over
sideways and bashful.
The boy throws a rock to him

The shell goes around and the
car turns over. The sunlight
is as clear as a
green bottle.

Man walking with his
shoulders haunched and tufts
of white duck hair in the back
of the head!   where were you born

The day is like splattered glass
The girls are wearing
bright sweaters and blouses.
They stop to let the cars pass

Life is green. Love is grey.
Purple are girls going to
school in wine jackets.

You stand at the corner of two
walls. Like handball
courts and a big bee
flies around you.

  There are many trees around
here. A bird flies crazily
  to one.
  Will he
  go in or not?

  A group of boys are waiting
to go in a yellow bus. A bird
down below flies over the
wall past me. Its front is blazing.

I am walking slowly. My feet
won't move. A rheingold truck
drives past me.

Rosemary is drinking
tea. Paul is running in his
sunsuit. The phone separates
us. They are eternal.
                    The phone is hot.

If you can imagine
a park, then you can
   see this crushed lollipop.

PART 2

I feel the cold peach
in my pocket. I am not
wearing a sweater.

Advance as I come to
you!   Alcohol comes to us.

Open your hand; the
fly springs away. The
air is cool on this spring-
board. The water must be cool.

Paul is watching me. His
eyes get sleepy with intensity.
He looks like he's
going to sneeze.

A whale was swimming near the coast last night.
The cement truck turns and I
realize how totally abandoned
all these workers are in their
easy happiness. But are they in
a combination of the wind?
I was looking all over for
                    you.

                Summer Dragon
A woman is walking. Her dress
is green as the grass and as
surprising. She has a hunched
back and her hair is
  grey like autumn grass
        and she walks
  looking down along the
grass lost and penetrating.
Is autumn

A Song

Why am I so dumb
now that you're gone;
now that you are gone?

The trucks behind me are
going at blasting power
A man walks toward
   me. The sun is blasting
the green shiny weeds
that are all around
            There is no one on the
            road. The road curves.
      I can't see where it goes
                  The bushes move but
                  the telephone pole doesn't

The roller goes over the
asphalt. The song "Love where
are you now, now that I need
you so" comes to me.
The roller goes over.

  But the rain falls down
and tatters away
my balls.

The whistle blows.
  Where are you now?
People cross the street
They are all carrying something.

What is this half feeding?
This half happiness
that hops at me
    last night?
    We picked you up last night
and you were beautiful,
the internal sunset
after the darkness
has stopped moving.
The plant that emits
a fragrance with all mothers.

In you, I feel
the new kite.
What are your feelings
                    like?

    O chemical and possible
flash,   The song goes
    on and on; the song.

PART 3

No mine is like
    the presents I want
      to give you:
wet lips, solar aches,
roadway dust, and
the rays of the moon
at the spots where they start.
I was born
before both of you
but like a man
I'm being withered
by you both
      into the dust
 of the moon
that you have brought
 back on your feet.
I see you both
and I am dispersed
like clouds mixing
like children skating.

Working writing and
decorating this star bright
misery. This pure
and lovely porto rican
waist. Where do
they work?

The little boys are fishing.
Just concentrating on hearing.
A sound of wheels squeaking
is in the trees.
Forever the sound goes on
like crickets, like night or
birds that call along
the highway and are barely
seen.
How long can I sit here?

Rest! The night is
being held by
 light droplets

 Ride your bicycle, my negro
green as the lake and
black as the trunks of trees.

I hear the train. I am
calling to the lake. "Goodbye."
 I turned my head fast.
I thought it was you at
a glance.
But it was a lady
carrying a fishing net.
She's younger than I thought.

A group of people touch
   me. What a life!
What a saw!
Charge me! oh silent
   zoo-bird.

I walk around this
leaf falling park
   Will I meet
someone I know, so far away?

Am I a Part of this
wheel of matter? just
because I am made of matter?
      I too disappear like solids;
. . . . . tomorrow night.

            The green lake is awake

 There are brown leaves
on the ground
   but I don't see even one
   in the full trees.

I was born a fluid.
The sun is shining on
half of the sign "Steel Pier."
   Magnifying.

The white duck is
blue along the water.
It skates slowly
  back and forth far
from me.
        My head will be warm
        because the air is warmer
        than the water.

I will see the duck like a baby
        coming towards me.

PART 4

It is time to go
  Love me! even when I falter.
The autumn leaves are
now beginning to start
falling.

I am awake: like
a colloid
just discovered in
        a breeze.

The truck woke me up.
        Assembling outside.

80

Two birds fly
over the street. They are on their way to some
  food. People are
continuing into their
building, to work.
    How friendly are
    those birds to
    each other?

The bee is coming closer to me.
It is like a flying object.

The duck is bobbing up and down.
It stays almost
in the same spot
as the water under it
moves away like a river.

The leaves are falling only
when the wind blows.
I have five minutes.

How I would like to just fall
asleep . . . . in the
movement . . . . . of all this
. . . . with you
near by me as I stretch
out my arm . . . . . .

with all these leaves
rolling across
                each other
Ditto, what suffering.
Accumulation.
Love,
degeneration, . . .
and regenerated dives

Every man or woman has
his own generator of love.

                    This autumn,
                    this autumn.
                    beard,
                    this autumn.

The crack in the wall
goes to the left
then to the right
continues down.
It stares at me.
It stares at us.
Paul is with us, you
are with us.
The stars are uncontrollable.

A woman is walking. The
muscle in her legs are
moving in slow gulps.

The gym comes
to my mind and the
smell at the beginning.
        It's
        so
        early.

PART 5

There's a match on
the floor; O bathroom of
stages! The sun burns through
the glass. It fortifies
the density of the leaves
and of your crying
last night.

I saw three girls
passing, going to work,
yet the whole street is
moving away.

The acorns are dry
The acorns are green
on the inside . . . .
        resonant as
        a testicle.

Oh cars, south breeze, two
people standing facing, truck,
baseball bat, swing, lint
flying around,
    go! on on on

Evening,
  I am holding the
ball, evening.

There is a new kite.
It is a bird kite.
It looks like a
bird.
It is made of stretched plastic.
No bird can
fly forever without
moving its wings.
The kite does not move
          its wings.
But there is a noise   coming from it

The electric motor new and
used is not like our brain
here in the darkness,
here in the morning black.

Take-ah, take- ah, tant, tant
    do-ah, do- ah
The bird goes in a tree.
    Bird goes
The bird goes
The pointed wings of
the seagulls
    practice on
pumping the skies.

        Orange soda.
        Distant voices.

How different each acorn
is here in his hand
here in the light, here in the
park   here in the light;
how different each
crumb is here in
        its beak